WEIRD LOOKING ANIMALS ON LAND AND ON THE SEA

SPEEDY
PUBLISHING

Speedy Publishing LLC
40 E. Main St. #1156
Newark, DE 19711
www.speedypublishing.com

The strange, bizarre and just plain weird looking creatures of the animal kingdom.

The lowland streaked tenrec is found in Madagascar. If they are threatened, they will give warning to their would be assailant by raising the spikes surrounding it's head and stomping their feet.

The komondor is a large, white-coloured dog with a long, corded coat. The Komondor's coat is long, and thick, about 20 – 27 cm long which resembles dreadlocks or a mop.

Proboscis monkeys get their name because of their long noses. The word means 'nose'. They are known to make loud honking sounds with the help of their long noses.

Wobbegong sharks can move across the ocean floor using their bottom fins. They are nocturnal, sleeping during the day and hunting at night, this is because they have poor eyesight.

The christmas
tree worm
is a colorful
marine worm
with beautiful,
spiraling plumes
that resemble a
fir tree. They are
commonly found
embedded in
entire heads of
massive corals.

Leafy sea dragons are called by this name as they have what looks like a leaf on their body. Leafy sea dragons are carnivorous species, they primarily feed on tiny crustaceans and plankton.

The narwhal is the unicorn of the sea. Male narwhals possess a great spiraled tooth that projects from their heads. The ivory tusk tooth grows right through the narwhal's upper lip.

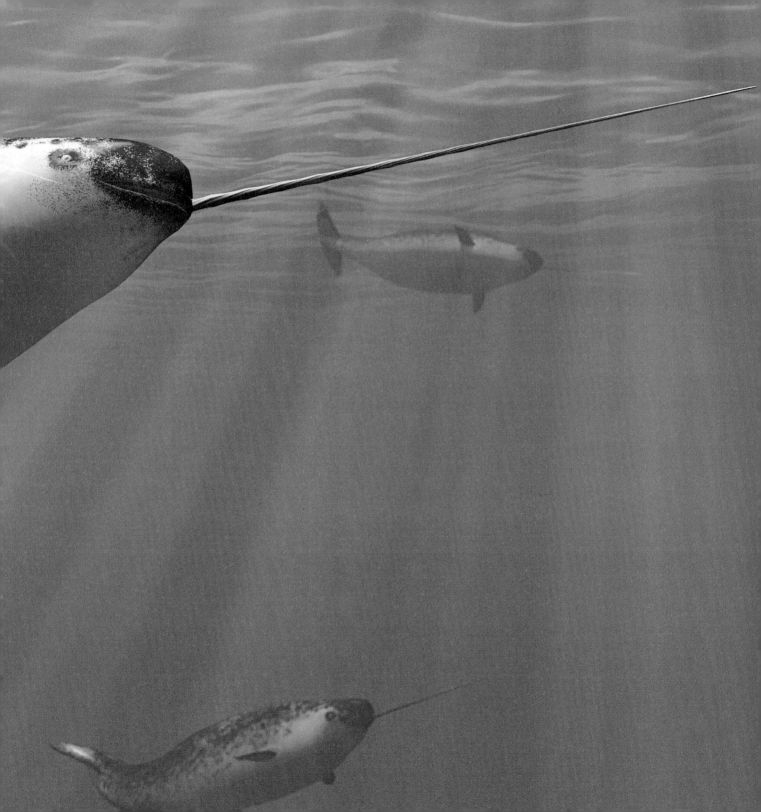

Made in the USA
San Bernardino, CA
01 October 2018